Data Protection Compliance in the UK

A Pocket Guide

Second edition

ROSEMARY JAY AND
JENNA CLARKE

IT Governance Pu

IT Governance Publishing
IT Governance Limited
Unit 3, Clive Court
Bartholomew's Walk
Cambridgeshire Business Park
Ely
Cambridgeshire
CB7 4EH
United Kingdom

www.itgovernance.co.uk

Pinsent Masons

First published in the United Kingdom in 2008 by IT Governance Publishing.

ISBN 978-1-84928-047-1 second edition 2010

(ISBN 978-1-905356-49-2 first edition)

FOREWORD

Secure management of personal digital information has become a key organisational challenge for both the public and private sectors in the 21st century's information age.

While headlines and news stories have been able to focus on a number of reported organisational failures to protect either personal or credit card data (or both), the reality is that there are many more organisations exposed to the sort of brand and market damage that prolonged negative headlines can have.

Regulators, of course, have their own view about the steps that organisations should be taking and, for all organisations operating in the United Kingdom; these include compliance at the very least with the requirements of Data Protection Act (DPA). Sanctions have become onerous and the potential penalties for non-compliance with the DPA are now significant. Other regulators (such as the FSA) are also taking steps to penalise organisations that fail to protect personal data, and these fines – as demonstrated by those imposed over the last few years – have been significant.

The Information Commissioner wants the DPA to go further than it does, and there is a growing expectation that breaches of the DPA will be automatically reported to the ICO.

Under these circumstances, everyone responsible for securing personal data within an organisation needs to have a practical understanding of their responsibilities under the DPA. Responsibility for securing personal data extends from members of the board through senior managers and functional heads to all those individuals whose job roles touch upon the security of personal data – irrespective of whether they collect, record, secure or despatch such data.

This pocket guide, written by the data protection experts at legal firm Pinsent Masons LLP, is specifically designed to provide everyone involved in the protection and security of personal data with a clear and lucid description of the contents of the DPA and what their responsibilities are in respect of securing that information. I hope that most organisations will not only ensure that this pocket guide is read by board members and senior management, but is distributed in large quantities to all those inside the organisation who have a role of any sort in respect of protecting and securing personal information.

Alan Calder

Ely, March 2010

PREFACE

All organisations now hold information about living individuals, and such information is almost always held on computer. As a result, everyone working in the public and private sector has to understand the proper way to handle this personal data. This pocket guide is intended for all employees, particularly directors, managers and IT teams, and gives an overview of how the law works.

The topics covered in this practical resource range from the UK Data Protection Act and EU regulations, the rights of individuals, security obligations, IT monitoring and interception to enforcement provisions and a good practice compliance checklist for staff.

It should be noted that the material included in this guide is accurate at the time of publication. However, detailed advice should be sought before taking any action.

Pinsent Mason's Information Law Team is independently recognised as one of the UK's leaders in data protection. Its clients include public and private sector organisations, which it advises on the full range of related legal areas.

Further advice may be found on *www.pinsentmasons.com* and *www.out-law.com*. OUT-LAW.COM is the IT legal advice and support service of Pinsent Masons LLP. It has been acclaimed as the leading e-commerce legal website in the UK and has won several legal industry awards. The service is based largely around the OUT-LAW.COM website which offers guides on all aspects of law relating to IT, e-commerce and new media, and a daily news service. The service is used by suppliers and users of technology in both the private and public sectors as a means of keeping up to date with developments in IT and e-commerce law. Through OUT-LAW.COM, Pinsent Masons is at the leading edge of IT law issues and has led the market in dealing with issues such as phishing and accessibility. The service currently has 39,000 registered users and is visited by 130,000 people each month.

ABOUT THE AUTHORS

Rosemary Jay is a partner with Pinsent Masons LLP. She heads the Information Law Team and advises public and private sector bodies on the law of data protection, privacy, access and surveillance. She is the author of Data Protection Law and Practice published by Sweet & Maxwell. Rosemary may be contacted via *rosemary.jay@pinsentmasons.com* or on +44 (0) 161 234 8374. Further information is available at *www.pinsentmasons.com*.

Jenna Clarke was a trainee with Pinsent Masons LLP at the time of writing. Her experience in the Information Law Team included advising and writing on data protection and freedom of information.

CONTENTS

CHAPTER 1: INTRODUCTION AND EU REGULATIONS

The Data Protection Act 1998[1] (DPA) came into force on 1 March 2000. It applies throughout England, Wales, Scotland and Northern Ireland. It is based on the EU Data Protection Directive of 1995[2] (DPD). Special rules cover the use of telecommunications data and the use of e-mail, telephone and fax for direct marketing. These are based on the EU Privacy and Electronic Communications Directive of 2002.[3] In the UK, this was implemented by the Privacy and Electronic Communications Regulations 2003[4] (PECR).

The DPA, like other legislation, has to be interpreted in the light of the Human Rights Act 1998.[5] This is particularly important for the DPA because the Human Rights Act includes a specific right relating to private life. This is Article 8 which reads:

1. Everyone has the right to respect for his private and family life, his home and his correspondence.
2. There shall be no interference by a public authority with the exercise of this right except such as is in accordance with the law and if necessary in a democratic society in the interest of national security, public safety or

---

[1] *www.opsi.gov.uk/acts/acts1998/ukpga_19980029_en_1.*
[2] *http://eur-lex.europa.eu/LexUriServ/LexUriServ.do?uri=CELEX:31995L0046:EN:HTML.*
[3] *www.ec.europa.eu/information_society/topics/telecoms/regulatory/new_rf/documents/l_20120020731en00370047.pdf.*
[4] *www.opsi.gov.uk/si/si2003/20032426.htm.*
[5] *www.opsi.gov.uk/acts/acts1998/ukpga_19980042_en_1.*

> the economic well being of the country, for the prevention of disorder or crime, for the protection of health or morals, or for the protection of the rights of freedom and of others.

The courts in recent years have used this provision to develop the law in the UK, so that it gives some protection for people's private lives even outside the scope of the DPA. This can be seen in the cases in which the court has decided that the publication of photographs of celebrity figures, such as Naomi Campbell, taken in private situations without their agreement has been a breach of confidentiality.

The Freedom of Information Act 2000[6] (FOIA) made some changes to the DPA for public authorities. As a result, people who seek access to information about themselves from public authorities will obtain more information than they would do from a private sector body. This is dealt with under the subject access provisions in Chapter 4.

The DPA will apply to an organisation if it is established in the UK and is responsible for personal data. If an organisation processes personal data in the UK but does not have an establishment in the UK then it will have to nominate a representative in the UK. The only organisations that will not be covered by the DPA are those that do not process any personal data or those that only use systems in the UK for the purposes of data transit through the UK.

---

[6] *www.opsi.gov.uk/Acts/acts2000/ukpga_20000036_en_1.*

Throughout the EU and the non-EU states (Iceland, Norway and Lichtenstein) in the European Economic Area (EEA), there are comparable rules on data protection, so information can flow freely among those countries. When information is to be sent outside that area, special rules will apply.

This pocket guide provides initial guidance to those who need to understand the Data Protection Act in the UK.

The information is intended to be for guidance only and is not authoritative. If an organisation has a specific legal query, it should seek specialist advice.

In this guide, we have also looked at the rules which cover monitoring telecommunications, for example the use of the internet by employees. These are covered by regulations made under the Regulation of Investigatory Powers Act 2000[7] but are so relevant to privacy concerns it is considered appropriate to cover them.

[7] www.opsi.gov.uk/acts/acts2000/ukpga_20000023_en_1.

CHAPTER 2: UNDERSTANDING THE DEFINITIONS

The DPA uses several specific terms and it helps to understand these. The DPA covers *personal data*. This means information which is held on a computer or in a relevant *filing system* and which relates to a living individual who can be identified from that information, or that and other information in the possession of the *data controller* (see below). It does not matter that the other information is held by a different department. Where public authorities are concerned, an even wider range of information is covered when it comes to dealing with rights of access to the information. If information is not held on a computer or a relevant filing system, or is not intended to be held on a computer or in a relevant filing system, then it will be outside the DPA, unless it is an accessible record. Accessible records are certain health, education or other public sector records formerly covered by other rights of access.

A relevant filing system is a set of manual files which are organised by reference to individuals or criteria relating to individuals (for example National Insurance numbers) and in which specific information about those individuals (for example their salary details or annual leave details) is 'readily accessible'. This usually means highly structured files in which the organisation can immediately find the information it seeks about a particular individual.

The term personal data was considered by the Court of Appeal in a case called *Durant v Financial Services Authority*[8] in 2003. This confirmed that a relevant filing system has to be tightly structured. The Court of Appeal also considered what sort of information can be said to 'relate to' a living individual. It decided that not all information in which someone's name is mentioned can be said to relate to somebody. The information has to be about them in some more significant sense, for example by being biographically significant.

There are very few organisations which do not process personal data about living individuals, whether that relates to employees, customers or suppliers. These individuals are called *data subjects*.

The organisation which determines the purposes for which such information is going to be used or processed and how this is going to be carried out is called a data controller. A data controller is the legal entity which is responsible for making those decisions. Employees are not data controllers even if they are data protection officers. If the information is held in the public sector, the public body will usually be the data controller, for example a local authority. Where information is held in the private sector, the data controller will usually be the company or other organisation, for example a limited company or a partnership. Every kind of use of personal data is covered by the DPA. The DPA defines any utilisation of

---

[8] *www.bailii.org/ew/cases/EWCA/Civ/2003/1746.htm*

personal data as *processing* and this covers everything from obtaining information in the first place through to storing it or destroying it at the end of its useful life.

Some types of information are regarded as more sensitive than others and these are called the *sensitive personal data* categories. The DPA sets out a list of categories of sensitive personal data which covers the racial or ethnic origins of individuals, their political beliefs, their religious beliefs, trade union membership, physical or mental health or condition, sexual life, or the commission of offences or criminal proceedings. Particular care has to be taken with such data, for example to make sure that it is held securely. Other important terms that are used in the DPA are:

- *Direct marketing*, which is widely defined as meaning the communication by whatever means of any advertising or marketing material which is directed to particular individuals.
- *Data processor*, which is any person apart from an employee of the data controller who processes data on behalf of a data controller.
- *Special purposes*, which mean the purposes of journalism and artistic and literary purposes.

CHAPTER 3: NOTIFYING PROCESSING WITH THE INFORMATION COMMISSIONER

Ever since the first Data Protection Act in 1984, those who process personal data have had an obligation to register on a public register. This is now called notification. There are some exemptions from this obligation. These are quite narrow: however, organisations will not need to notify if the only reasons they process personal data are for what are called the core business purposes. These cover marketing, staff administration and accounting, but care should be taken when relying on these and reference should be made to the Information Commissioner's website[9] and the guidance available. Notification lasts for a year.

From 1st October 2009, there has been a two-tier fee structure. Data controllers must pay a fee of £500 if they are either a public authority with 250 or more members of staff, or a private sector body with a turnover of £25.9 million and 250 or more members of staff. Others pay only £35.00. The details will be put onto a public register that can be accessed on the Information Commissioner's website. To notify you must provide:

- the name and address of the organisation;
- the name and address of the representative if one has been nominated;

[9] *www.ico.gov.uk.*

- a description of the personal data which is being processed and the category or categories of data subjects;
- a description of the purposes which data are to be processed;
- a description of any recipients; and
- the names or description of places outside the EEA to which personal data are to be transferred.

The organisation must also describe its security measures in general terms, although this information is not included on the register. Data controllers have an obligation to make sure that their register entries are kept up to date. If they fail to do this, they may be guilty of a criminal offence. The DPA provides for some types of processing to be subject to prior checking by the Information Commissioner but this has never been brought into operation. Even if a controller does not have to register (because they are within one of the narrow exemptions), they have to be prepared to make the same information available to a member of the public who asks for it.

Organisations should be aware of bogus agencies requesting payment for data protection registration, as these agencies are not connected to the Information Commissioner's Office and often charge a fee exceeding the standard notification charge.[10]

---

[10] See the Information Commissioner's guidance for small businesses: www.ico.gov.uk/upload/documents/library/data_protection/practical_application/getting_it_right_a_brief_guide_to_data_protection_for_smes.pdf.

CHAPTER 4: WHAT ARE THE RIGHTS OF INDIVIDUALS?

The DPA provides individuals with some important rights. These are:

- the right of subject access;
- the right to object to direct marketing;
- the right to object to processing in some circumstances;
- the right to object to automated decision making;
- the right to rectification of inaccurate data; and
- the right to compensation.

In addition, under the PECR, data subjects can decide to register on the Telephone Preference Service (TPS).[11]

Subject access

If a data subject makes a written application to a data controller, he or she is entitled to be told whether the controller has any personal data about that individual; and if so, to receive a description of the information held and an explanation of the purposes for which it is processed. Most importantly, the data subject must be provided with a copy of the information about themself. It should be noted the data subject is not entitled to a copy of the actual documents or printouts but to a

[11] www.mpsonline.org.uk/tps/.

copy of the information which is contained in that material. A data controller does not have to respond to an access request unless they receive a request in writing which gives sufficient information for them to verify the identity of the individual and to find what is being requested. The data controller can also charge a fee up to £10.

The definition of personal data is wide and can cover e-mails, digital sound recordings, CCTV films as well as relevant filing systems. This may require a wide range of information to be searched, although in *Ezsias v Welsh Minsters*[12] the judge held that a data controller is only required to make a 'reasonable and proportionate search' to find the information requested. Where the data controller is a public sector organisation, it also has to search and give information from all its manual files, subject to some special rules:

- The subject has to describe unstructured information so the organisation can find it.
- The individual cannot have his or her manual personnel records; and
- If it would take longer than 18 hours to find the information (or 24 hours if it is a government department), the request can be refused.

In responding to a request, the data controller must consider whether to remove or 'redact' information that relates to other living individuals. The controller must consider whether they have agreed

---

[12] Ezsias v Welsh Ministers [2007] All ER (D) 65 (Dec) High Court.

to the disclosure of the information about them, the importance of the information, and whether any duty of confidentiality is owed to the third party. However, if the data controller judges it sufficiently important to the data subject, the data controller may choose to provide such information.

The right of subject access generally overrides other prohibitions on disclosure. There are, however, some circumstances in which subject access need not be given, including where to do so would prejudice the prevention or detection of crime, apprehension or prosecution of offenders, would cause problems with national security or where the information is subject to legal professional privilege. In addition, exemptions apply which are intended to protect vulnerable data subjects and allow information about physical or mental health conditions or about social work to be withheld. These are subject to specific rules and have to be signed off by appropriate professionals. Care should be taken when seeking to apply any of these exemptions.

Where information is already publicly available, for example on the electoral role, then the individual cannot exercise a right of subject access in relation to it.

A data controller has 40 days within which to respond to a subject access request. A person who considers him or herself aggrieved by a failure to obtain subject access can either complain to the Information Commissioner or has the right to go to court and ask the court for an order requiring the controller to provide the access requested. A court looking at such a request is entitled to see all of the information in order to decide whether or not it should have been disclosed.

Objection to direct marketing

A data subject is entitled to object to his or her personal data being processed for the purposes of direct marketing. If an organisation receives such an objection, it must act on it and stop sending the material. Data controllers are usually advised to suppress names: that is, put a marker against the name showing that the individual does not wish to be marketed, rather than removing a name from a list. If a name is removed from a list there is always the concern that it may be added back in without the organisation realising that this is the name of a person who has already lodged an objection.

There is also a service called the Mailing Preference Service (MPS).[13] This service is run by the Direct Marketing Association[14] and individuals can opt out of marketing by direct mail by registering on the stop list. Members of the Direct Marketing Association must check their marketing list against the stop list so that people who have registered with the MPS do not receive unwanted mail. There are additional rules for e-mail, fax and telephone marketing which are covered in Chapter 9. These apply in addition to the general right to object to marketing.

---

[13] *www.mpsonline.org.uk/mpsr/.*

[14] *www.dma.org.uk/content/home.asp.*

Objection to processing

Where a data controller processes personal data for purposes other than direct marketing, an individual can raise some objections but these are more limited. As an example, if a data controller is processing in order to perform a contract with the data subject or because the data controller is under a legal obligation to process, then the right to object does not apply. A data subject who wants to object to processing must lodge a written objection with the controller. They have to show that the processing in question is causing, or is likely to cause, substantial damage or substantial distress to themself or another, and that this is not outweighed by the legitimate interests of the data controller in carrying out the processing. Relatively few objections to processing are lodged but where they are, the individual does not have to refer specifically to the DPA, so data controllers should be alert in recognising these. A data controller who receives such an objection has 21 days within which to respond and either agree or disagree. The data subject who is not happy with the response can ask the court to make an order telling the controller to stop processing.

Objection to automated decision making

Automated decisions are decisions which significantly affect an individual and are based solely on the processing by automatic means of personal data about that data subject. Examples given in the DPA are decisions made for the purpose of evaluating matters, such as performance at work, credit worthiness, reliability or conduct. The decision must significantly affect the individuals. An individual can either object before the processing takes place and require the data controller to take a decision by a non-automated means, or they can object after the processing has taken place and ask for the decision to be revisited. A data controller which takes automated decisions which fall within this section must notify the data subject of this as soon as is reasonably practicable after the decision was taken.

Again, if an individual is not satisfied with the way their rights have been handled, they have a remedy by going to court.

Rectification

The courts are given wide powers to deal with information which is shown to be inaccurate. They can order that the record be put straight or that additional information be added to a record. Equally they may require a data controller to 'block' data so that others cannot see it, or to erase or destroy inaccurate records.

An individual who wants the court to exercise these powers must apply to the court and show that the information is inaccurate within the terms of the DPA; that is, that it is incorrect or misleading as to any matter of fact.

Compensation

Individuals are entitled to compensation if they have suffered damage because a requirement of the DPA has been breached by a data controller. The individual has to show that damage has been suffered. This means either physical damage or some tangible financial loss. It is not enough that the individual has suffered from hurt feelings or embarrassment. However, where the complaint is that the data controller has been processing information that is being used for the special purposes (that is, journalism, art or literature) in breach of the DPA, then damage is not needed and distress alone can be a ground for action. The Information Commissioner cannot award compensation; the individual must go to the courts.

It should be noted that these rights are quite significant. The one most often used by data subjects is the right of access, and organisations should be alert in recognising and dealing with subject access requests within the 40-day timescale.

CHAPTER 5: UNDERSTANDING AND APPLYING DATA PROTECTION PRINCIPLES 1 TO 6

The rules for how personal data must be processed are found in the eight data protection principles. One of the principles deals with security and another with overseas transfer; these are dealt with in separate chapters. In this chapter, we look at principles 1 to 6:

- Principles 1 and 2 deal with the basic rules for allowing processing of personal data to take place and the restrictions on what data controllers can do with the data.
- Principles 3, 4 and 5 deal with data quality.
- Principle 6 deals with the rights of data subjects.

Principle 1 requires a data controller to process personal data fairly and lawfully. It imposes a restriction on any processing unless the data controller can satisfy one or more of the conditions set out in Schedule 2 and, for sensitive personal data, Schedule 3 to the DPA. Schedules 2 and 3 are important provisions. They set out lists of conditions for processing. The Schedule 2 conditions apply to all personal data and every data controller must be able to point to one or more of these to justify its grounds for processing. The Schedule 3 conditions only apply to sensitive personal data. If sensitive personal data are processed, the controller must also show a Schedule 3 condition.

There are six grounds for processing in Schedule 2. The ones most commonly relied upon are that:

- the data subject has given his consent to the processing;
- the processing is necessary for performing a contract with the data subject;
- the processing is necessary for complying with a legal obligation imposed on the controller other than under a contract;
- the processing is necessary for public functions; and
- the processing is necessary for the legitimate interests of the controller or others and there is no unwarranted prejudice caused to the rights and freedom, or legitimate interest, of the individual.

The final ground is potentially wide and the Information Commissioner has accepted that this is the case.

As would be anticipated, the Schedule 3 grounds are more detailed. There are a large number of Schedule 3 conditions because they have been extended by statutory instruments, in particular the Data Protection (Processing of Sensitive Personal Data) Order 2000,[15] but some common grounds for processing sensitive personal data are that:

- the data subject has given explicit consent;
- the processing is required for the purposes of complying with employment law;

---

[15] *www.opsi.gov.uk/si/si2000/20000417.htm*

- the processing is necessary for legal advice or legal proceedings; and
- the process is necessary for medical purposes and is undertaken by health professionals.

In all cases the grounds for processing are set out in full in the Schedules. Data controllers should have careful regard to these and ensure that they have an appropriate ground for processing any personal data and in particular for processing sensitive personal data. These grounds can be quite restrictive and careful consideration may be needed.

As well as setting out the requirement to have grounds for processing, principle 1 imposes an obligation on controllers to make sure that data subjects receive proper information about what will happen to the personal data that relates to them. Where information is obtained from a data subject, or about a data subject from a third party, the controller must make sure that the following information is provided to the data subject:

- the identity of the data controller;
- the identity of any nominated representative of the data controller;
- the purposes for which the data controller intends to process the data; and
- any further information which is necessary to ensure that the individual is being treated fairly.

This information is often provided in the form of a data protection notice. Such notices are seen in application forms or in websites or may be given orally. It is particularly important that any non-obvious uses or disclosures of information are described to individuals. In some circumstances, the notice also provides information and offers options to individuals about e-mail or other marketing under the PECR. Under the PECR, individuals must not be sent fax marketing or marketing by e-mail unless either they agree or, in the case of e-mail, some specific provisions apply. Individuals are also given the right to opt out of telephone marketing by using the TPS or by notifying the organisation directly. Data Protection Notices from commercial organisations often include a range of notifications and options in relation to types of marketing and disclosures to third parties for marketing. This is not, however, the only purpose of such notices and care must be taken to ensure that notices offer all relevant information to individuals. There are some unusual circumstances where data subjects need not be given a full notice (for example when information is being collected in the course of a criminal investigation and to tell the individual would prejudice that investigation) but in most cases notice should be provided.

The requirement to give a notice is part of the obligation to make sure that processing is carried out fairly, but this is not limited to the notice. Data controllers must ensure that they are being fair to individuals in their uses of personal data. Principle 1 also requires that personal data should be processed lawfully. This is a very general term which covers matters such as ensuring that organisations do not breach any other laws such as confidentiality or copyright when they process personal data, or ensuring that public bodies have a proper basis for any activity they carry out.

Principle 2 says that personal data should be obtained and processed only for specified and lawful purposes and not further processed in a way incompatible with those purposes. The purposes are specified both in the register of notification and in the notices given to data subjects. Once the data controller has notified the purposes for which they intend to use the data, they will be restricted to those uses and those which are compatible to the original purpose. If a data controller wishes to use personal data for a new and incompatible purpose, they would be expected to seek the consent of the individuals to the new use. In many cases, however, the new uses will be compatible with original notified uses, particularly in the commercial sphere, and it may be sufficient for the controller to tell the individual of the changed or additional use. In some circumstances, they should, however, give the data subject an opportunity to opt out of the use for the new purposes.

Data quality principles

Principles 3, 4 and 5 deal with obligations to ensure that personal data is adequate, relevant and not excessive for the purposes of the processing, is accurate and, where it is appropriate, kept up to date, and that it is not be kept for any longer than is necessary for the purposes. These principles can be met by adopting proper records management procedures. In particular, data controllers should have retention schedules setting out how long information will be kept for particular purposes, and proper processes to delete information when it is no longer needed. Data controllers should not simply collect information without having a clear view of how it will be used, and should keep all information collection under review. There are some additional rules about accuracy. If a data subject notifies a data controller that they consider the data about them to be inaccurate, then the controller should investigate that and, where there is a disagreement, indicate that this is the case on the record. There are special rules for information held by credit reference agencies where there is a dispute about accuracy.

Principle 6 on the rights of data subjects

Principle 6 states that personal data shall be processed in accordance with the rights of data subjects. As we have seen in Chapter 4, data subjects have a number of important rights and are entitled to have recourse to the courts to enforce these rights. However, a data subject may also complain to the Information Commissioner. The Information Commissioner can investigate and can take enforcement action because such a breach will also be a breach of principle 6.

CHAPTER 6: SECURITY OBLIGATIONS AND DATA PROCESSORS

Principle 7 is an important provision of the DPA. It states that data controllers must take appropriate technical and organisational measures against unauthorised or unlawful processing of personal data and against accidental loss or destruction of or damage to personal data. The DPA explains what should be weighed in deciding whether security measures are appropriate. The data controller has to consider the harm that might result from the unauthorised or unlawful processing or accidental loss or destruction or damage to data and the nature of the data to be protected, and must ensure an appropriate level of security taking into account the state of technology and the cost of implementing security measures. The Information Commissioner generally refers to ISO27001 as an appropriate security standard which could be adopted by data controllers to help meet their obligations.

Another aspect of principle 7 is that the data controller must take reasonable steps to ensure the reliability of employees who have access to personal data. This generally means that the data controller must ensure people are properly trained and will be subject to disciplinary action if they fail to comply with the company's proper security standards.

Where a data controller decides to use a third party to process personal data on their behalf (a data processor), then specific arrangements must be entered into with the processor. When choosing a data processor, the data controller must make sure that the processor can offer sufficient guarantees of security to look after the data, and must take responsibility for ensuring that the processor complies with those measures. This usually means that where any data processing is outsourced, data controllers require security standards to be set out in writing, reserving the right to audit or inspect the processing.

A further formal requirement is for there to be a contract between the parties either made or shown in writing under which the data processor must act only on the instructions of the data controller and which imposes equivalent security obligations to those set out in the principle. It is common for data controllers to use third-party processors, for example if they have outsourced their back office functions. Data processor clauses should always be included in such contracts and care should be taken to ensure they cover all the relevant requirements. Breaches of security may give rise to penalties under other provisions. (The Nationwide Building Society was fined nearly £1 million by the Financial Services Authority when one of its staff had a laptop stolen from his car.) Clauses with data processors may be in a stand-alone agreement but may be incorporated into larger contracts. These should make clear which of the parties is the controller and which is the processor and set out the obligations of the processor to process only in accordance with the instructions of the controller. Data controllers will also want to ensure that they are notified of any security breach, have rights to audit the security arrangements and that, at the end of any contract, the processor returns all the personal data to the controller and does not retain any of the information.

CHAPTER 7: TRANSFERRING DATA OVERSEAS

Principle 8 is another important provision. It limits the transfer of personal data to countries outside the EEA unless the data controller can bring themself within one of the exceptions to this prohibition, or they can be sure that equivalent protection is provided for the personal data in the country to which it is being sent.

Simply putting information on a website hosted within the EEA does not amount to a transfer of personal data, but if information is deliberately pushed onto a website outside the EEA or is transferred, whether electronically or by disc or other mechanism outside the EEA, or access is given from outside the EEA, then these provisions apply.

The restrictions on sending personal data outside the EEA have broad implications for businesses which trade internationally and for organisations which use outsourced providers in other jurisdictions.

Several countries have been accepted by the European Commission as offering equivalent protection. The European Commission is entitled to make such judgments under its powers under the DPD and all the member states of the EU must accept these rulings. The countries which have been named so far include Argentina, the Isle of Man, Guernsey, Jersey, Switzerland and Canada, although Canada is not covered for all personal data. Although the USA has not been recognised by the EU as having general law which provides equivalent protection, there is a special arrangement with the USA under which US companies can adopt self-regulatory standards equivalent to EU law and, if they do so, enter what is called Safe Harbor.[16] The standard of self-regulation must meet the rules of Safe Harbor and the US company must validate that its behaviour complies with these standards.

Where personal data is being sent to a jurisdiction which is not approved, it will have to consider other justifications for the transfer. Schedule 4 sets out a list of cases where the prohibition does not apply. These exceptions apply:

1. Where the data subject has given their consent to the transfer.
2. Where the transfer is necessary for performing a contract with the data subject.
3. Where the transfer is necessary for performing a contract with, or for the benefit of, the data subject.
4. Where the transfer is for reasons of substantial public interest.
5. Where the transfer is necessary for or in connection with legal proceedings or advice.
6. Where the transfer is to protect the vital interests of the data subject.

[16] *www.export.gov/safeharbor/.*

7. Where the transfer is of personal data on a public register.
8. Where the terms of the transfer have been approved by the European Commission or authorised as being made in such a way as to provide for adequate protection for personal data.

The first seven of these are self-explanatory, although a business that wishes to rely upon any one of them should review the detailed wording of the provision in the DPA. The eighth deals with transfers being made in accordance with 'approved terms'. This is a reference to the use of European Commission-approved model contracts for transfers. The European Commission has accepted that where two parties enter an agreement which binds the parties to ensure the proper protection of the personal data, this can be a solution to the problem of transfer where the data protection law in the receiving jurisdiction would be inadequate. The European Commission has gone on and approved model contracts for use in these circumstances.

There are two model contracts which deal with controller-to-controller transfers, and one model contract which deals with controller-to-processor transfers. The controller-to-processor contract has been amended, and the new version must be used for all contracts entered into after 15th May 2010. If an organisation uses a model contract, the European Commission and the national regulator anywhere in the EU must accept that this meets an appropriate standard of adequacy. If these contracts are used, the controller or processor must adopt the contract as it stands.

As the rule is that personal data should not be transferred to a country outside the EEA, unless that country provides for an adequate level of protection, another option is for a data controller to make an assessment of the adequacy of the level of protection rather than relying on an exception or one of the mechanisms for transfer. In doing so, the controller must take account of the provisions in the DPA which explain the relevant considerations in determining adequacy. The data controller must have regard in particular to:

- the nature of the personal data;
- the country or territory of origin of the information;
- the country or territory of final destination of the information;
- the purposes of the processing and the period for which the data are to be processed;
- the law in force in the relevant country or territory;
- the international obligations of the country or territory;
- any relevant codes of conduct or practice which are enforceable in the territory; and
- any security measures taken in relation to the data in that country.

The task of making an assessment of adequacy is a difficult one for most data controllers and there is a tendency to rely upon the use of one of the other mechanisms, particularly the model form contracts.

A more recent innovation has been the introduction of Binding Corporate Rules (BCRs)[17] as a mechanism to allow transfer. These can be used by global companies with a group structure to pass information among the group. Under BCRs, all of the group companies both within and outside the EEA, between which data will be transferred, sign up to a common set of self-regulatory rules dealing with the relevant personal data. These rules are then agreed and signed off by the relevant EU regulators. This is quite a complex process and only a few examples have as yet been approved.

Overseas data transfers outside the EEA pose an area of difficulty for many data controllers and if an organisation has a considerable number of global transfers care should be taken to ensure that whatever scheme is adopted is both appropriate and robust.

[17] *www.ico.gov.uk/what_we_cover/data_protection/international/international_transfers.aspx.*

CHAPTER 8: APPLYING EXEMPTIONS

The DPA imposes a regime which controls the processing of personal data and imposes obligations on the data controller to provide information to individuals. In Chapter 4, the exemptions to the obligation to provide subject access were noted. The data controller may also be relieved from the obligation to provide notice to individuals in certain circumstances. The exemptions only apply on a case by case basis. A data controller who plans to rely on these should make a proper record of the justification for doing so. In other circumstances, restrictions on disclosure are lifted so that a disclosure may be made even though in normal circumstances it would not be permissible. These include circumstances where information is required for the purposes of journalism or legal proceedings, where information is disclosed in order to deal with regulatory activities, or where the national security or policing exemptions apply. Information which is held by individuals solely for their personal purposes, family or household affairs, is not covered by most of the provisions of the DPA.

Information may also be used for research, even if it was not originally obtained for that purpose.

Exemptions are technical and only apply on a case by case basis, so care should be taken when relying on them.

CHAPTER 9: MARKETING USING ELECTRONIC METHODS

PECR includes special rules for marketing by fax, e-mail and telephone. Faxes for marketing purposes must not be sent to individual subscribers unless those subscribers have agreed to receive them. Corporate subscribers may opt out by registering with the Fax Preference Service.[18] They also have the right to notify the marketer that the organisation does not wish to receive marketing faxes.

Telephone marketing must not be carried out to any subscriber, whether a corporate subscriber or an individual subscriber, who has either told the caller that they do not want to receive such calls, or that they have registered with the TPS.

There is no restriction (apart from complying with the general data protection rules) about sending e-mail marketing to people at their work or corporate e-mail address, but marketing e-mails to individual subscriber addresses is restricted. Marketing e-mails can be sent to individual subscribers if those subscribers have agreed to receive them or in the limited case that the sender has obtained the details in the course of a sale or negotiation with the individual, has provided an opportunity to opt out of direct marketing when the communication details were initially collected, and where the person is marketing similar products and services only. An opt-out opportunity has to be given at each time of marketing.

---

[18] www.mpsonline.org.uk/fps/.

In all of these cases, the person using or instigating the electronic service used to send the marketing must ensure that their identity and information about how they can be contacted are made available to the individuals.

These regulations also impose special rules in relation to the use of information by electronic service providers and the use of cookies or other electronic mechanisms for gaining access to subscribers' data. These rules apply as well as the rules imposed by the Electronic Commerce (EC Directive) Regulations 2002[19] and the Consumer Protection (Distance Selling) Regulations 2000.[20]

---

[19] *www.opsi.gov.uk/si/si2002/20022013.htm.*
[20] *www.opsi.gov.uk/si/si2000/20002334.htm.*

CHAPTER 10: IT MONITORING AND INTERCEPTION

The monitoring of electronic communications and the interception of the content of calls is a serious issue for most businesses. Monitoring is the activity of listening to calls while they are taking place but not keeping an electronic record; interception is both listening and keeping a record, that is, taking a copy or retaining a copy of the call. Communications data is the information generated as a result of calls showing the numbers called, time spent on the call and other information about the call.

An organisation's IT policy should make clear that monitoring will take place, if this is the case and set out when the content of communications may be intercepted. This can be lawfully carried out by an organisation, if both parties to the call consent, or under rules set out in the Telecommunications (Lawful Business Practice) Interception of Communications Regulations 2000[21] (LBPR), made under the Regulation of Investigatory Powers Act 2000 Section 4(2).[22] All organisations should ensure that any interception takes account of the LBPR otherwise they may find that the interception has been challenged as unlawful. The Information Commissioner gives guidance on monitoring in the Code of Practice on Employment[23] purposes and advises that less

[21] *www.opsi.gov.uk/si/si2000/20002699.htm.*
[22] *www.opsi.gov.uk/acts/acts2000/ukpga_20000023_en_1.*
[23] *www.ico.gov.uk/Home/for_organisations/topic_specific_guides/employment.aspx.*

intrusive mechanisms should be used for monitoring where possible: for example, communications data should be considered first. If there is then cause for concern, monitoring or interception may take place under the LBPR.

Users of a system must be told of any monitoring and interception and it may only be carried out by the person with the right to control the lawful operation or use of a system. Any interception on a public system is a criminal offence, but under the LBPR the person who controls a private system is entitled to intercept on that private system as long as it is limited to communications by means of which transactions are entered into in the course of business or take place in the course of a business. All those who use the communication system should be notified. This includes those who may telephone into a system. The system controller may monitor in order to ascertain compliance with regulatory or self-regulatory practices, in the interests of national security, for the purposes of preventing or detecting crime, or for the purpose of investigating or detecting the unauthorised use of the system. In addition, they may monitor communications to determine whether they are relevant to the system controller's business or where those are made to a confidential voice telephony counselling or support system. Any organisation considering utilising monitoring should have specific regard to the detailed provisions of the LBPR and ensure that they are complied with.

CHAPTER 11: ENFORCEMENT PROVISIONS

The DPA is enforced by the Information Commissioner who is also responsible for the FOIA. Among other roles, the Commissioner issues codes of practice. Most recently, the Commissioner has revised the code of practice for the use of CCTV, and issued a draft code covering data protection on line. The Commissioner's website also provides useful guidance on a whole range of topics. The Information Commissioner has an obligation to maintain the register and to provide advice on the DPA.

An individual, who is aggrieved because they believe there has been a breach of the DPA or of the PECR, may complain to the Information Commissioner and ask that an assessment of the processing is carried out. At the end of the assessment process, the Commissioner will usually make a decision about whether there has been a breach or not. The Commissioner does not have to receive a complaint, but may act where he or she considers the circumstances warrant it. The Commissioner has a number of statutory powers, including the power to serve an Information Notice to require a data controller to provide them with information. The recipient can appeal to the Information Tribunal, which is a special tribunal set up to deal with appeals under the DRP and the FOIA. The Commissioner can also go to court to obtain a warrant which enables entry to premises to investigate. Warrants are not used as a matter of routine, but are sometimes applied for where there are possible criminal offences.

The Commissioner may serve an enforcement notice on a data controller who has not complied with the data protection principles. The notice will set out how the data controller has contravened the DPA and what must be done to set matters right. Again there is an appeal against such a notice to the Information Tribunal. A notice can cover a wide variety of matters, and may require a data controller to change the way that their systems work, or to stop using information in particular ways, or to alter the notices that they give to individuals.

From April 2010, the Commissioner will be able to impose fines of up to £500,000 on data controllers who commit serious breaches of the DPA which are likely to cause substantial damage or distress to individuals. The breach must be deliberate, or reckless, and recipients may appeal to the Information Tribunal.

The Coroners and Justice Act 2009 also amended the DPA to give the Commissioner the power to carry out compulsory assessments of government departments. Before doing so, they must serve an Assessment Notice on the department, setting out how they propose to exercise their powers.

CHAPTER 12: PENALTIES FOR NON-COMPLIANCE

Some actions give rise to criminal proceedings under the DPA. The most serious of these is the offence under Section 55 of obtaining or disclosing personal data, or procuring the disclosure of personal data without the consent of the data controller. In order to commit the offence, the accused must know or be reckless that they do not have such consent. There are various defences, including the possibility that, in the particular circumstances, the activity was justified in the public interest. The Information Commissioner has recommended that this offence should carry a custodial sentence, and it is likely that the law will be changed accordingly. Currently the offence is punishable by a fine of up to £5,000 in the Magistrates' Court, or an unlimited fine in the High Court.

Offences are also committed if notification is not kept up to date, or if an enforcement notice is breached. It is an offence to intercept a communication in the course of transmission by a public telecommunications service. Breach of the data protection principles is not currently an offence in itself but, if an enforcement notice is served and ignored, may eventually give rise to criminal liability.

Criminal offences can be committed by both data controllers and by individual employees or others. If the failure to comply with the DPA is shown to be the act or default of an officer or manager, then that officer or manager may be prosecuted along with the company. A court considering a criminal matter can also order the destruction of personal data. This has been done on at least one occasion.

CHAPTER 13: COMPLIANCE CHECKLIST FOR STAFF

This checklist is intended as a good practice guide for staff (particularly those in the IT section). It is not a general checklist for the organisation as a whole.

- Know who the data protection officer is in your organisation, so that queries can be raised with the appropriate person.
- Check that your registration with the Information Commissioner covers everything for which your section is responsible and, if there are any gaps, ensure your data protection officer is alerted to this.
- Be aware of those circumstances in which personal data may be collected by your section or your business unit, and check that all of those points of collection have data protection notices that comply with your organisation's policy.
- If you are responsible for special services, such as the website or setting up marketing e-mails, ensure you are up to date on the relevant rules and are wholly compliant.
- Check what training is available within the organisation for staff on data protection security and related issues. Make sure that you have attended any appropriate training and take responsibility for other people in your section.

- Be alert for any changes in business practice and ensure that your processes and procedures take account of these.
- Make sure that you and those in your section are aware of security and confidentiality rules and that these are applied stringently. In particular, do not leave passwords around, ensure that any personal data on laptops is securely encrypted and that there are rules to restrict the movement of laptops which hold personal data.
- Be vigilant to ensure that personal data cannot be stolen or removed from your offices by the use of mobile storage (for example, USB keys).
- Check that there are proper guidelines in place to cover disclosures of information and make sure that no inappropriate disclosures are made, particularly in response to telephone calls.
- Ensure that you and any staff for whom you are responsible follow security guidance on disclosures and do not make disclosures of personal data outside the rules.
- Be aware of the rights which individuals have in relation to their personal data and, in particular, be alert for subject access requests or objections to processing where the individual does not need to say that they are acting under the DPA.
- Alert your data protection officer to any changes in business practice that would impact on your compliance, for example the use of a new processor where a processing contract

would be required or a request to transfer personal data outside the EEA where you need to ensure that there are proper provisions in place.

- Be aware of the retention procedures in operation and ensure that data are not kept longer than necessary for the purposes of your section or unit.
- If any systems use an automated decision-making process, be alert to objections and recognise that individuals should be notified of the use of such systems.
- When you record information about individuals, ensure that it is appropriate, adequate, correct and fair. Do not record unverified or inadequate information.
- Do not allow staff to make marketing telephone calls or send marketing e-mails without having checked that your organisation is compliant with the appropriate rules.
- Ensure that you respond swiftly and professionally to any communications from the Information Commissioner's Office.

APPENDIX: ABBREVIATIONS

DPD	EU Data Protection Directive of 1995
DPA	Data Protection Act 1998
EEA	European Economic Area
EU	European Union
FOIA	Freedom of Information Act 2006
LBPR	Telecommunications (Lawful Business Practice) Interception of Communications Regulations 2000
MPS	Mailing Preference Service
PECR	Privacy and Electronic Communications Regulations 2003
TPS	Telephone Preference Service

ITG RESOURCES

IT Governance Ltd. sources, creates and delivers products and services to meet the real-world, evolving IT governance needs of today's organisations, directors, managers and practitioners. The ITG website (*www.itgovernance.co.uk*) is the international one-stop-shop for corporate and IT governance information, advice, guidance, books, tools, training and consultancy.

www.itgovernance.co.uk/data-protection.aspx is the information page from our website for data protection resources.

Other Websites

Books and tools published by IT Governance Publishing (ITGP) are available from all business booksellers and are also immediately available from the following websites:

www.itgovernance.co.uk/catalog/355 provides information and online purchasing facilities for every currently available book published by ITGP.

www.itgovernanceusa.com is a US$-based website that delivers the full range of IT Governance products to North America, and ships from within the continental US.

www.itgovernanceasia.com provides a selected range of ITGP products specifically for customers in South Asia.

www.27001.com is the IT Governance Ltd. website that deals specifically with information security management, and ships from within the continental US.

ITG Resources

Pocket Guides

For full details of the entire range of pocket guides, simply follow the links at *www.itgovernance.co.uk/publishing.aspx*.

Toolkits

ITG's unique range of toolkits includes the IT Governance Framework Toolkit, which contains all the tools and guidance that you will need in order to develop and implement an appropriate IT governance framework for your organisation. Full details can be found at *www.itgovernance.co.uk/ products/519*.

For a free paper on how to use the proprietary Calder-Moir IT Governance Framework, and for a free trial version of the toolkit, see *www.itgovernance.co.uk/calder_moir.aspx*.

There is also a wide range of toolkits to simplify implementation of management systems, such as an ISO/IEC 27001 ISMS or a BS25999 BCMS, and these can all be viewed and purchased online at: *http://www.itgovernance.co.uk/catalog/1*

Best Practice Reports

ITG's range of Best Practice Reports is now at *www.itgovernance.co.uk/best-practice-reports.aspx*. These offer you essential, pertinent, expertly researched information on an increasing number of key issues including Web 2.0 and Green IT.

Training and Consultancy

IT Governance also offers training and consultancy services across the entire spectrum of disciplines in the information governance arena. Details of training courses can be accessed at *www.itgovernance.co.uk/training.aspx* and descriptions of our consultancy services can be found at *http://www.itgovernance.co.uk/consulting.aspx*. Why not contact us to see how we could help you and your organisation?

Newsletter

IT governance is one of the hottest topics in business today, not least because it is also the fastest moving, so what better way to keep up than by subscribing to ITG's free monthly newsletter *Sentinel*? It provides monthly updates and resources across the whole spectrum of IT governance subject matter, including risk management, information security, ITIL and IT service management, project governance, compliance and so much more. Subscribe for your free copy at: *www.itgovernance.co.uk/newsletter.aspx*.